limpet

cockle

murex

bottom-shell

episcopal mitre-shell

textile-cone

First Published in 1970 by
Macdonald and Company
(Publishers) Limited
St. Giles House
49-50 Poland Street
London W1

Managing Editor
Michael W. Dempsey B.A.

Chief Editor
Angela Sheehan B.A.

Made and printed in Great Britain
by A. Wheaton & Company
Exeter Devon

MACDONALD FIRST LIBRARY

By the Sea

Macdonald Educational
49-50 Poland Street
London W1

cliffs

groyne

marram grass

sand

2

The sea-shore is the place where the land
meets the sea.
There are different kinds of sea-shore.
Some sea-shores are sandy.
Some are muddy.
Some are rocky.
Some sea-shores have cliffs on them.

The flat part of the sea-shore is called
the beach.
Many plants and animals live on the beach.

tide in

The height of the sea changes during the day.
We call the changes tides.

Twice each day the level of the water rises.
The sea covers the sand and the waves crash
against the rocks.
The tide is in.

Twice each day the level of the sea falls and
the tide goes out.
The rocks and the seaweeds on the beach
are uncovered.

Many animals can be found on the beach when
the tide is out.

tide out

dry seaweed

worm-cast

sandhopper

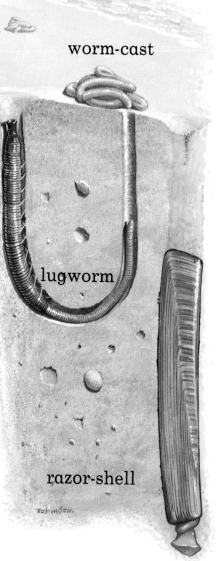

cockle-shell

lugworm

A sandy beach looks empty
when the tide is out.
But it is not really
empty.
There are lots of
animals in the sand.
They bury themselves
to keep away from the
hot sun.

razor-shell

6

The razor-shell can bury
itself very quickly.
It uses a special foot to
bury itself in the sand.

foot   shell

sand

The razor-shell's foot
does not look like a
man's foot.
It looks more like a
tongue.

The razor-shell digs its
foot into the sand.

Then the foot pulls the
shell right down into
the sand, until it is
completely hidden.

7

Pools of water are left on a muddy beach
when the tide goes out.
There are stones and seaweed on the beach
as well.

When the tide goes out, some animals are
left in the pools.
Some animals bury themselves in the mud.

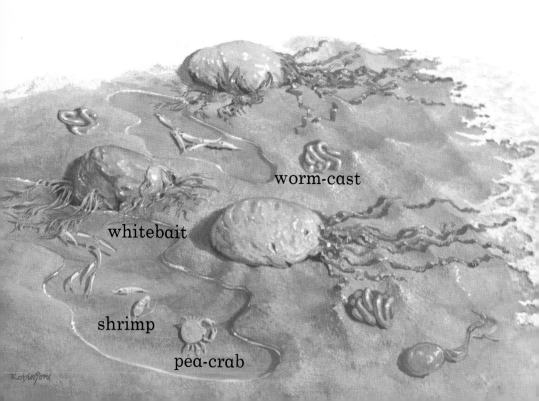

worm-cast

whitebait

shrimp

pea-crab

Shrimps live in the sea.
They may be left in a
rock-pool when the tide
goes out.

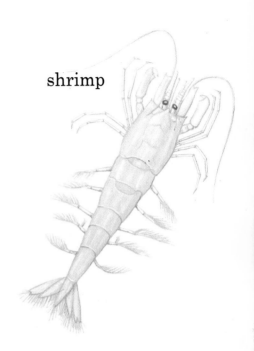

shrimp

Shrimps can dart about
very quickly.
They go pink when they
are cooked.

The pea-crab is a very
small crab.
It is the same size as
a pea.
It lives inside the
shells of dead mussels.
It eats dead shrimps
and bits of dead fish.

pea-crab

grass

Scots-lovage

sea-campion

sea-lavende[r]

thrift

puffin

The seaweeds and lichens that grow on the beach
do not have flowers.
The plants on the cliffs do have flowers.
Some of the flowers grow on the steep sides of
the cliff, and some in pebbles at the bottom.

Sea birds make their nests on the cliffs.
Some birds make their nests on ledges.
Some make their nests in holes.

sea-holly

yellow-horned
poppy

lichen

11

It is easy to find animals on a rocky
sea-shore.
The animals cannot bury themselves, as the
animals on sandy beaches can.
If you sit and watch a rock-pool you will
see the animals crawling or swimming about.
You can see sea-anemones, limpets,
periwinkles and barnacles.

The rocks may be covered
with barnacles.
A barnacle has a
trap-door in the top of
its shell.
When the tide is in it
opens the door and
puts out its legs to
catch food.

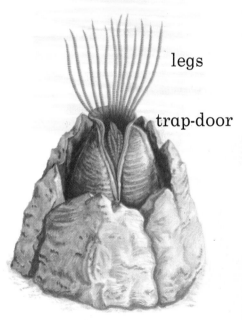

legs

trap-door

sea-anemone

Sea-anemones are strange animals.
When the tide is in they open like flowers.
When the tide goes out they close up.
They look like little blobs of jelly.

red seaweed

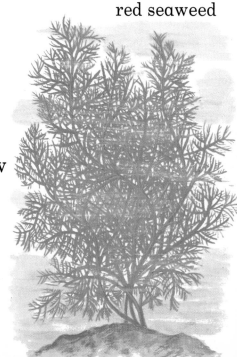

This pretty red seaweed often grows in rock-pools.
Green seaweeds and brown seaweeds also grow on the sea-shore.
Many animals eat seaweed.

Winkles are found on
rocky sea-shores.
They hide in cracks
in the rocks when the
tide goes out.
Winkles also hide under
stones and in seaweed.

winkle

blenny

Sometimes fishes are
left behind in rock-
pools when the tide
goes out.
They hide among the
seaweed in the pool.
If you move the seaweed
the fish will dart out.

15

When the tide goes out you can see lots of seaweed on the beach.

Sometimes there is so much seaweed that you cannot see the rocks.

sea-lettuce

Sea-lettuce grows on
rocky sea-shores.
It grows on the part
of the beach which is
uncovered when the tide
goes out.

Some seaweeds can only
grow under the water.
Even when the tide goes
out this brown
tangleweed is not
uncovered.
It grows on stones on
sandy beaches.
You can often find
tangleweed on beaches
after a storm.

tangleweed

bladder-wrack

Some seaweeds are called wracks.
This is bladder-wrack, or 'pop weed'.
The swellings on its leaves pop if they are squeezed.

periwinkle

Many animals, such as these periwinkles, hide in the bladder-wrack when the tide goes out.
They hide so that the sun will not dry them up.

18

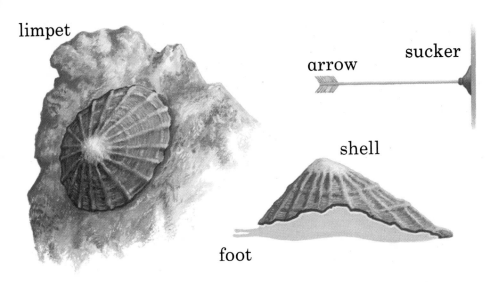

limpet

arrow

sucker

shell

foot

This animal is a limpet.
It lives on rocky shores.
Limpets cling to the rocks very firmly.
It is very hard to pull a limpet away from
its rock.
The limpet has a round foot that holds it
tightly to the rock.
The sucker on the end of an arrow sticks to
a tile in the same way.

19

There are many fishes in the sea but it is hard to see them.

It is much easier to see the fishes which are left behind in rock-pools when the tide goes out.

This fish is a rock-goby.

When it is left in a rock-pool it hides among the seaweed or beneath the rocks.

rock-goby

ballan-wrasse

The ballan-wrasse is
quite a large fish.
It lives among the
tangleweeds near the
beach.
You can often find
sea-scorpions in
rock-pools.

sea-scorpion

21

shore-crab

claws

This is a shore-crab.
It lives under stones and in rock-pools.
The shore-crab is an angry crab.
French people call it the angry-crab.
When it is disturbed it waves its claws.
It snaps its claws on its food.

The hermit-crab is not
like other crabs.
It does not have its own
hard shell.
It lives inside the shells
of dead sea-snails.

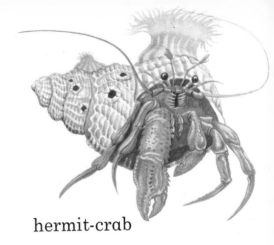

hermit-crab

Spider crabs have very
long, thin legs.
They live in rock-pools.

The little edible-crabs
live on the beach in the
summer.
In the winter they go
out to deeper water,
where the big crabs live
all the time.

spider-crab

edible-crab

23

Worms are hard to find because they bury
themselves and hide under the stones.
Spirorbis is a worm which lives in tiny round
tubes on the seaweed.
The tubes look like little white circles
on the seaweed.

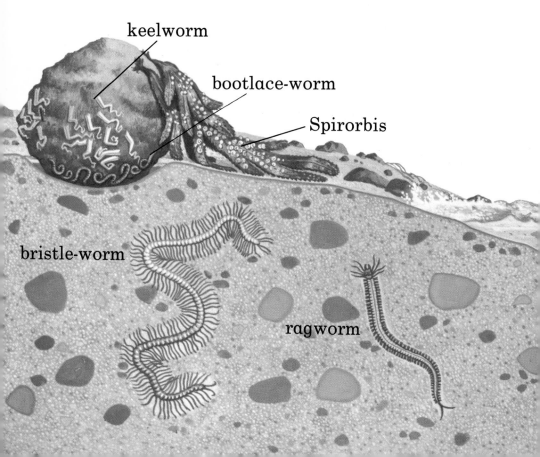

keelworm

bootlace-worm

Spirorbis

bristle-worm

ragworm

We cannot see these worms because they
stay inside their tubes.
Keelworms live on stones.
When the tide is in and the water covers the
beach the peacock-worm comes out of its tube.
It catches its food with its long tentacles.

The sea-mouse is very pretty.
It has rainbow colours on its hairy body.

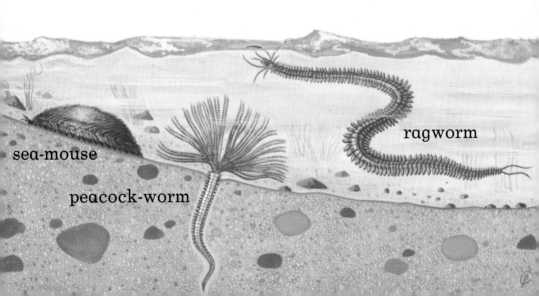

sea-mouse

peacock-worm

ragworm

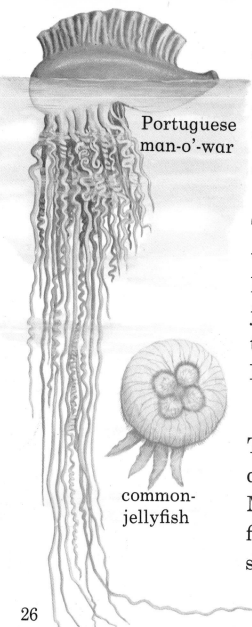

Portuguese
man-o'-war

common-
jellyfish

Jellyfishes float in the sea, and catch their food with their tentacles. They have stings on the end of their tentacles.

The Portuguese man-o'-war is very large. It is really lots of small jellyfishes joined together. It has a nasty sting.

The common-jellyfish is a small jellyfish. Many common-jellyfishes float together in a shoal.

Starfishes and brittle-stars live on the bottom
of the sea.
Sometimes starfishes and brittle-stars are
washed up on the beach.

Sea-urchins also live in the water.
They walk about on their long spines.

Starfishes and brittle-stars and sea-urchins
all have spiny skins.

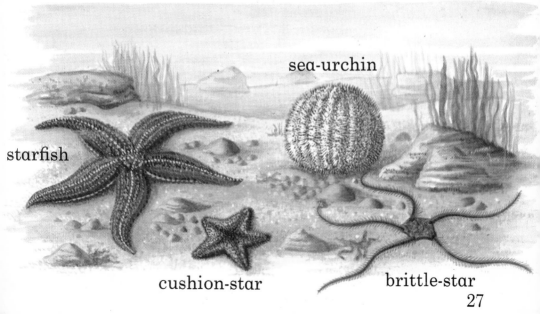

sea-urchin

starfish

cushion-star

brittle-star

herring-gull

Many birds live by the sea.
The herring-gull is seen on most sea-shores.

oyster-catcher

The oyster-catcher wades
on the flat shore when
the tide is out.

It eats the shellfish
and worms buried in the
sand and mud.

Some sea birds dive into the sea to catch
fishes for food.
Gannets dive into the water from high in
the sky.

Cormorants dive into the water from rocks.
When they come out of the water they spread
out their wings to dry.

gannet

cormorant

When sea-snails die their shells are washed
up on the beach by the waves.
There are many different kinds of sea-snail.
Each kind has a different shell.
Some beaches are made of sea-shells instead
of sand.
Every sea-shore has some shells on it.

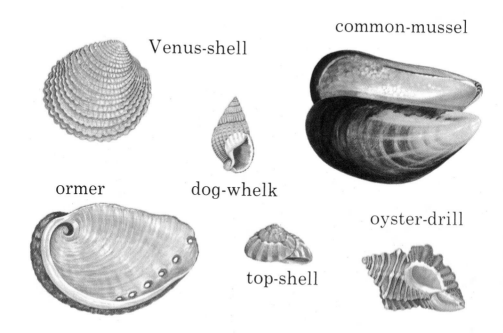

Venus-shell

common-mussel

ormer

dog-whelk

oyster-drill

top-shell

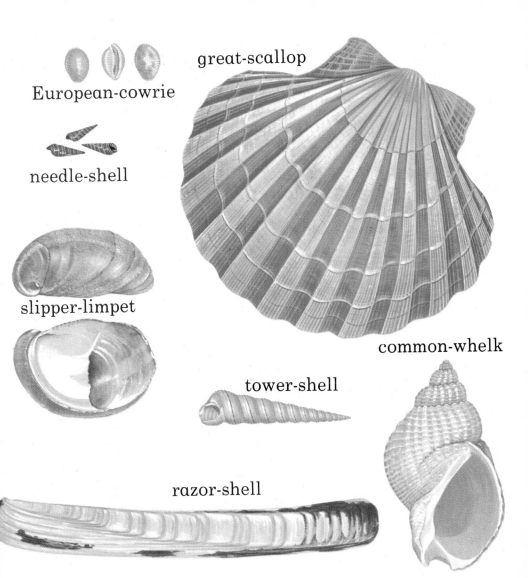

European-cowrie

needle-shell

great-scallop

slipper-limpet

tower-shell

common-whelk

razor-shell

31

Index

MACDONALD FIRST LIBRARY

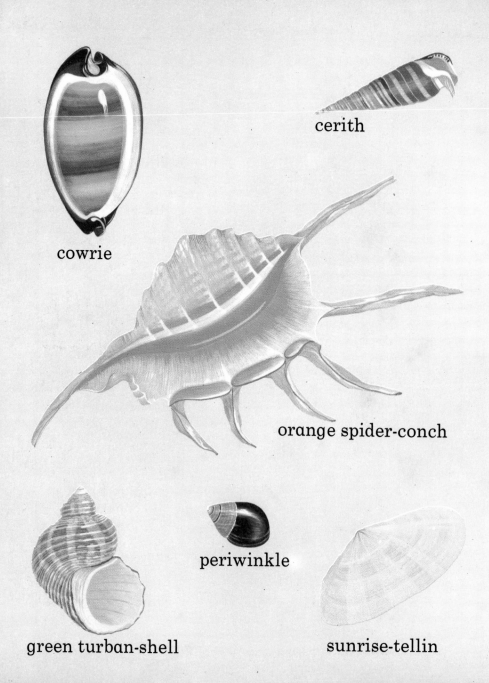

cowrie

cerith

orange spider-conch

green turban-shell

periwinkle

sunrise-tellin